This is a book about growing

For Sara O. – M. J.

For Louis, Elliot & Ayla – H. T.

First published 2018 by Walker Books Ltd, 87 Vauxhall Walk, London SE11 5HJ

This edition published 2019

2 4 6 8 10 9 7 5 3 1

Text © 2018 Martin Jenkins

Illustrations © 2018 Hannah Tolson

The right of Martin Jenkins and Hannah Tolson to be identified as author and illustrator respectively of this work
has been asserted by them in accordance with the Copyright, Designs and Patents Act 1988

This book has been typeset in Kreon

Printed in China

British Library Cataloguing in Publication Data: a catalogue record for this book is available from the British Library

ISBN 978-1-4063-8271-6

www.walker.co.uk

WALKER BOOKS

AND SUBSIDIARIES

LONDON • BOSTON • SYDNEY • AUCKLAND

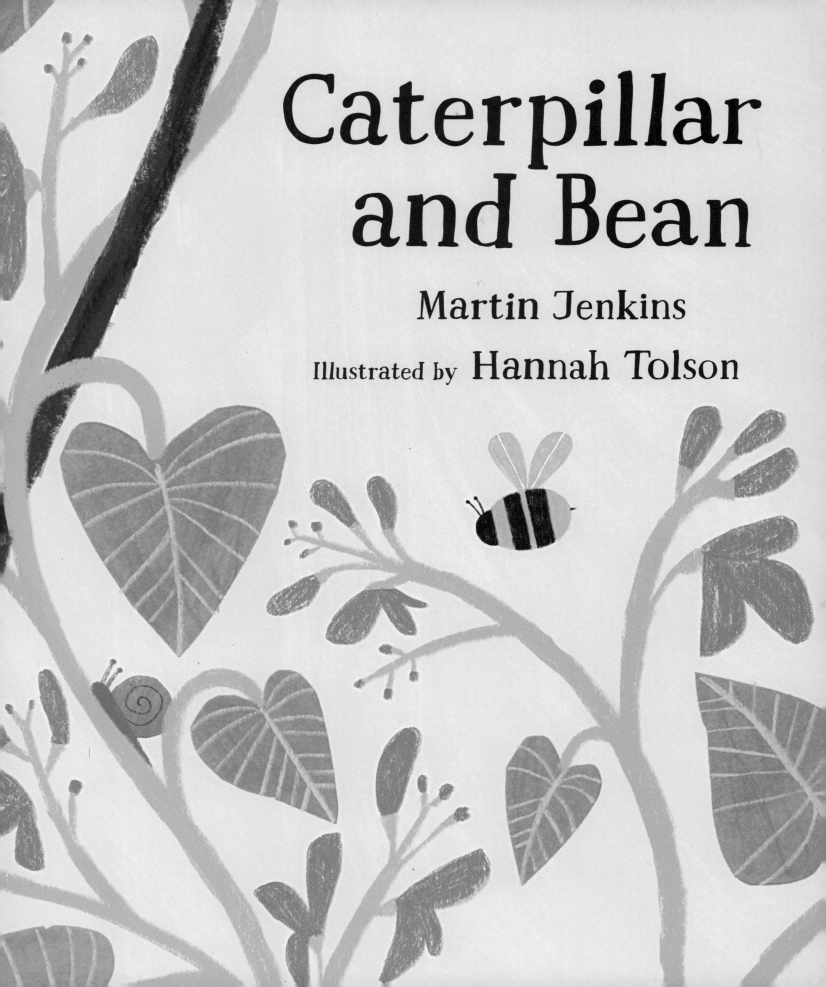

Caterpillar and Bean

Martin Jenkins

Illustrated by Hannah Tolson

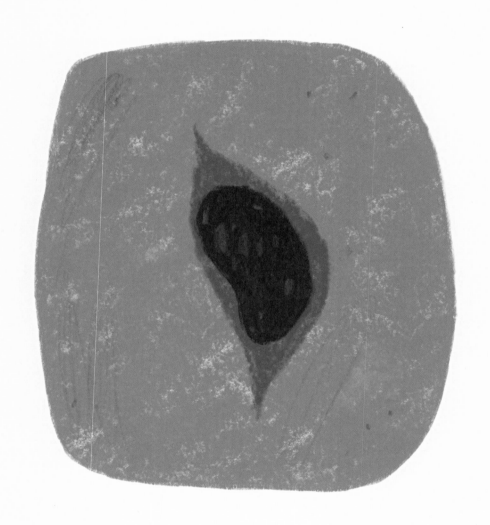

What's that wedged in a crack in the ground,
small and hard and wrinkly and brown?

A bean seed.

Seeds need water to grow.

Now here comes the rain splashing down,
running into the crack in the ground.

The seed has swollen and its skin has split.
There's something white poking out.

A root.

The root has pushed down into the ground.
Two new things have appeared,
green and round.

Leaves.

water and chemicals from the ground for the plant.

The roots get water and chemicals from the ground for the plant.

These leaves were folded away inside the seed.

The bean plant needs sunlight to grow.

The sun is shining after the rain.

More leaves have grown.

These ones are different.

There's a little white dot on one of the leaves.

How did it get there? What is it?

An egg.

There are holes in the leaf where the egg used to be.
Something's been busy. I wonder what?
Whatever it was, it hatched from that dot.

A caterpillar.

The caterpillar must have been hungry –

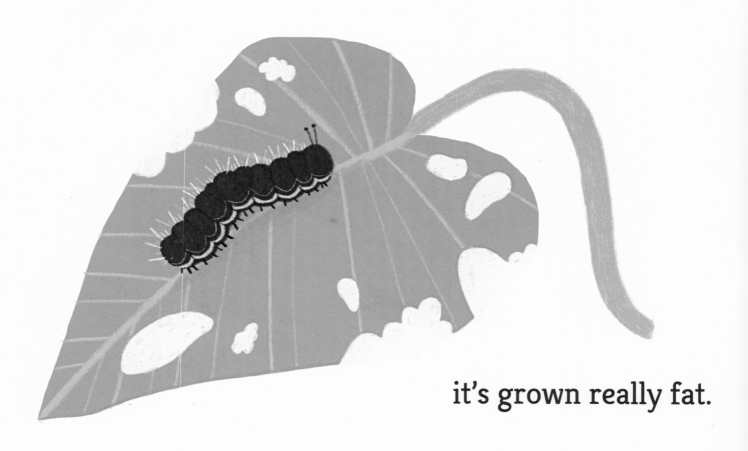

it's grown really fat.

Now it's bursting out of its skin.
But there's a new skin underneath.

The caterpillar grows out of its skin three times, getting bigger each time.

Goodness.

There's hardly a leaf left on the poor plant.

Do you think it's going to be OK?

New leaves have grown.
That's a relief!

The bean plant needs its leaves to
be able to go on growing.

Now the plant has really grown big.
And it's got flowers.
And to think it all grew from a wrinkled
brown seed that was wedged in a crack.

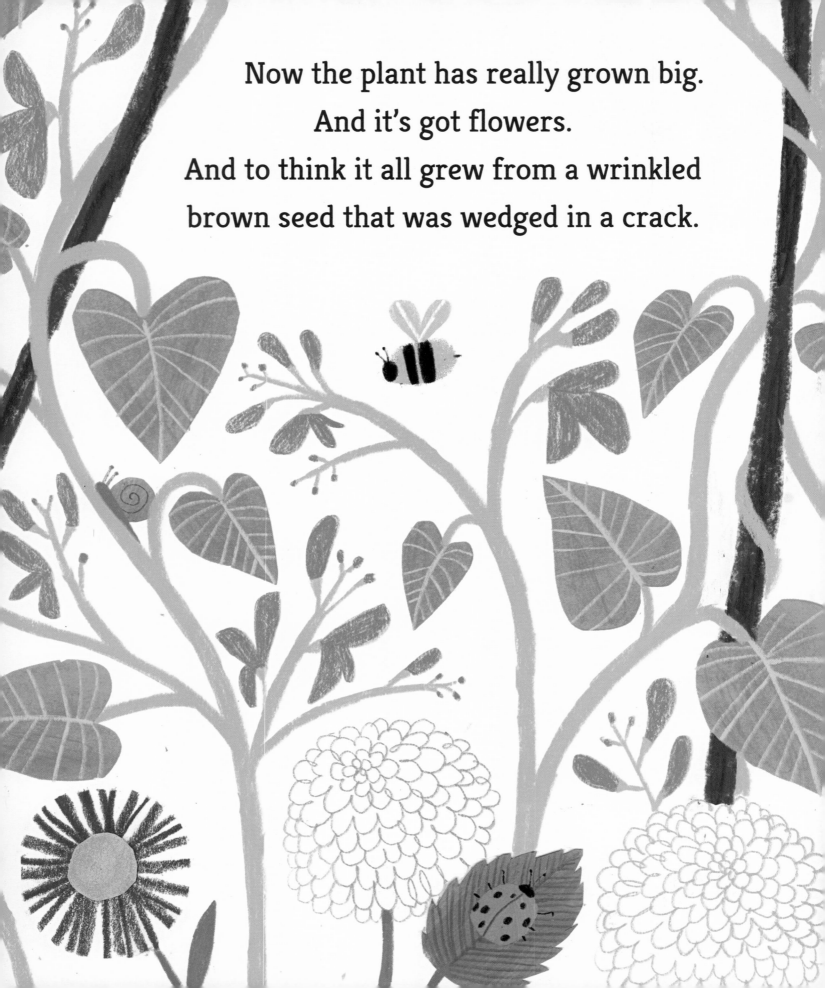

Inside the chrysalis the caterpillar
dissolves into a kind of soup.

But where is the caterpillar?
Has it died?
No, it's turned into a chrysalis,
hanging down on a thread.

Green pods are forming
where the flowers used to be.

They've grown longer and fatter. They're drying
out fast. Soon they'll split open and out will tumble …

bean seeds, all wrinkly and brown, some of which might end up in cracks in the ground.

The bean plant dies in the winter, leaving its seeds behind.

And what about the chrysalis?
All through the winter it hangs by its thread.

Then one warm day in spring,
it splits apart and out comes …

a beautiful butterfly,
looking for somewhere to lay her eggs!

Grow your own bean plant

First get some bean seeds. Scrunch up some kitchen paper and put it in a clean jar. Pour in enough water to make the paper damp but not sopping. Push the seeds down between the paper and the side of the jar. Put the jar on a windowsill and keep the paper damp – you may have to add a little water nearly every day.

What happens to the seeds? What comes out first? Which way does it grow? What happens next? How long does it take? If the beans go on growing (sometimes they get diseases and die), you can plant each in a flowerpot full of soil or compost.

INDEX

Look up the pages to find out about growing. Don't forget to look up both kinds of word, this kind – and **this kind.**

BIBLIOGRAPHY

Here are some other books about growing:

Caterpillar Butterfly by Vivian French, Walker Books (2016)

Oscar and the Frog by Geoff Waring, Walker Books (2008)

Growing Frogs by Vivian French, Walker Books (2015)

More Science Storybooks:

ISBN: 978-1-4063-8270-9

ISBN: 978-1-4063-8252-5

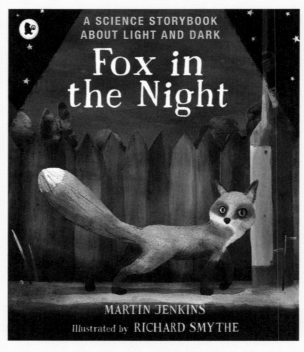

ISBN: 978-1-4063-7975-4

This **Walker book belongs to:**